CONTENTS

KT-160-254

YOUR DOG
FROM HEAD TO TAIL

Dogs evolved from an ancient breed of wolf and were probably the first animals to be tamed. They started living with people more than 15,000 years ago, when they gave them early warnings of intruders and helped hunters by sniffing out and chasing prey.

Claws: Strong, blunt claws grip the ground as the dog runs and they are also used for digging.

Tail: The tail gives a good clue as to how a dog is feeling.

Legs: Powerful leg muscles allow dogs to run long distances.

Feet: Dogs only have sweat glands in their paws, so they have to cool down by panting.

Eyes: Dogs cannot see as many colours as we can, but they have better vision in dim light.

Ears: A dog can hear a sound four times farther away than a human can and they hear high sounds that we cannot.

Brain: The part of a dog's brain devoted to smelling is 40 times larger than that of a human's.

Nose: Dogs have up to 300 million scent receptors, compared to six million in a human nose. They have a special scent detection organ, called the Jacobson's organs, in the roof of their mouth.

Whiskers: These detect air movements and vibrations, and warn of obstacles in the dark.

Mouth: Sharp teeth and strong jaws are adapted for attacking prey and tearing at food.

DOG FACTS

- Bloodhounds can track a human scent over great distances. In 1954, a bloodhound found a missing family by following a trail that was 12 days old.

- Dogs may take 300–400 breaths per minute when they're panting to cool off.

ALL SHAPES AND SIZES

Dogs vary in size and shape more than any other pet. Big or small, long-distance runner or couch potato, pedigree pup or mixed-breed, there will be a dog out there that's just right for you. Here are just a few of the many popular breeds.

Cocker Spaniels were bred for hunting birds. They are eager to please, playful and active – and they usually get on well with other pets.

Dachshunds were bred with short legs to hunt badgers and other burrowing animals. They like to bark and can be mischievous.

Greyhounds are sprinters and don't need huge amounts of exercise – in fact they spend a lot of time sleeping. They are bred to chase prey, so need to be kept on a lead when out for walks.

Dalmatians were bred to run alongside carriages so they need plenty of exercise. They are intelligent but need careful training.

Newfoundlands are strong swimmers thanks to their webbed feet. They are hard-working dogs that once pulled nets for fishermen.

Yorkshire Terriers are little dogs with big personalities. They love to play, but they may bite if small children are too rough with them.

Great Danes are gentle giants. Their sweet nature makes them perfect pets, but their huge size means they won't fit into every home.

GREAT AND SMALL

- One of the smallest-known adult dogs was a Yorkshire Terrier that was 9.5 cm long and weighed just 113 grams.

- One of the largest-known dogs was an English Mastiff that weighed in at 155.6 kg and was 250 cm from nose to tail.

Labradors are friendly and intelligent. They need a lot of exercise and are easily bored. They love food and can become overweight.

CHOOSING YOUR DOG

Before you choose a dog, think about all the things you'd like to do with your new pet. Dogs have been bred to do all sorts of jobs and this affects the way they behave. Some are clever and want lots of attention, others love to run and need plenty of exercise.

PUPPY OR ADULT DOG?

If your family is happy to put up with chewed-up shoes and toilet-training in exchange for hours of fun, then a puppy is right for you. Otherwise, there are lots of older dogs looking for new homes, and they will probably already be neutered and toilet-trained.

PEDIGREE OR MIXED BREED?

If you get a pure-breed puppy, you'll know what to expect when it grows up, but a tiny mixed-breed pup may become a massive adult. As dogs come in all sizes, ask about the puppy's parents so you have an idea of how big your dog is likely to grow.

LARGE OR SMALL?

Think about the space in your home and imagine a large dog there. Would you still have room to move around? Most large dogs need more exercise than smaller breeds and they cost more to feed. Smaller breeds usually live longer than big dogs.

MALE OR FEMALE?

If your puppy has been neutered, there's little difference between male and female dogs. Males may be larger, while females grow up more quickly and can start training at a younger age.

WALKIES!

Be realistic about the amount of time you can spend walking your dog and don't choose a breed that needs longer walks than you have time for. Surprisingly, a Great Dane needs about the same amount of walking as a Jack Russell Terrier, so size isn't always a guide.

IN THE DOG HOUSE

Puppies are always getting into mischief, so puppy-proof your home to make sure there's nothing harmful within reach before you collect your dog.

A dog crate will keep your pet safe when you're out of the room, and it's a place for your puppy to rest when it needs a break. A crate that fits in the car will be useful when you take your pet on trips, or to see the vet.

If you can bring back some of your puppy's old bedding, it will feel more at home.

PET CHECK ✓

Does your dog have:

- somewhere cosy to sleep?
- food and water bowls?
- toys?

A water-resistant mattress makes a comfortable bed.

UNDERSTAND YOUR PET

I may be happier on your lap in the back of the car than inside a carrier on the journey home.

Puppies are champion chewers, so get some chew toys to save your shoes from those sharp little teeth.

You'll need a collar, lead and ID tag so your dog can get used to them before going outside.

STOCK UP ON SUPPLIES

It's best to offer your dog the same food it is already used to eating. If you want to switch to another food, do it gradually by replacing a little of the original food at a time. You'll need ceramic or stainless steel bowls for food and water and some treats for training.

A grooming brush and flea comb will keep your dog's coat in good condition, and grooming can help to build a bond between you and your pet.

GETTING TO KNOW YOU

WELCOME HOME

Show your pet its sleeping area and then let it explore its new surroundings. Dogs like company, so make sure your pup gets plenty of attention and, if you have a crate, keep it close to the centre of family life.

Bring your dog home at a quiet time and don't leave it alone for long periods during the first few weeks. It's good to introduce your pet to lots of people, but give your new friend a few days to settle in before inviting visitors round.

BEDTIME

Dogs normally sleep with their pack so your pup will probably want to spend the first night with one of the family. If you don't want your dog sleeping in the bedroom, a hot water bottle and a ticking clock wrapped in a blanket placed in its bed may help to reassure it.

RULES RULE

Dogs love routines so set one up as soon as your dog comes home. It will feel more secure if it knows the house rules from the start. Other family members must stick to them too, so agree on a list before your new pet arrives.

UNDERSTAND YOUR PET

Please don't try to give me a hug. Dogs don't like being held tightly and I might bite.

MEETING OTHER PETS

Shut other pets in a separate room when your dog first comes home. When you introduce them, keep one animal on a lead, in a crate or behind a pet barrier so they can get used to one another without any risk. Make sure your pets have become good friends before leaving them alone together.

DOGGY DIETS

Dogs are happy to eat the same food every day and sudden switches can cause stomach upsets. Don't disturb your dog while it's eating and never feed it from the table – your dog wouldn't like you to take its food so don't let it share yours.

Dried food is useful if you have to leave it out during the day.

FEEDING PUPPIES

Puppies need four meals a day at eight weeks old and three meals a day between 12 weeks and six months because they are growing so fast.

FEEDING DOGS

Adult dogs need two meals a day. Meaty dog food is closest to their natural diet and it has everything they need to stay healthy. Dogs should always have a bowl of fresh water nearby, but clear away any left-over food.

UNDERSTAND YOUR PET

I'll eat anything, so please make sure I can't get at food that could make me ill.

These human foods are dangerous for dogs:

- chocolate
- grapes, raisins and sultanas
- onions, garlic and chives
- pecans, walnuts and macadamia nuts
- avocados
- salt and some artificial sweeteners
- coffee and alcoholic drinks

PLUMP POOCHES

Wild dogs are scavengers and eat anything they find, even if they're not hungry. Pet dogs are the same so it's important to keep food out of reach. Overweight pets have a lot of health problems, so don't give in to those pleading puppy eyes.

TREATS

If you reward your dog with treats during training, give it less food at the next meal. Treats should be no bigger than your fingernail.

DAY-TO-DAY CARE

Help to make sure your dog stays fit and well by keeping a look out for any unusual behaviour or signs that your pet might be in pain.

If a dog stops eating, that's usually a clue that something is wrong.

GROOMING

Dogs don't do much to keep themselves clean and some do their best to get dirty. Grooming your pet regularly keeps its coat and skin in good condition.

UNDERSTAND YOUR PET

It may be good for me to have a bath and get my teeth cleaned, but that doesn't mean I have to like it!

BATHING

Dogs are quite happy to be dirty and stinky, so they'll do their best to avoid a bath. You can help to make it fun for them with lots of toys and treats. Use lukewarm water and dog shampoo, and don't get water on your dog's face or in its ears. Be prepared to get wet!

NAIL CLIPPING

A dog's nails need to be clipped once a month, or your pet could suffer a lot of pain – just like you if you never had your toenails cut. Remind an adult when it's time to do it.

DOGGY DENTAL CARE

By brushing your dog's teeth a few times a week, you can stop your pet suffering painful tooth and gum problems. Let your dog lick some dog toothpaste from your finger and touch its teeth with a soft brush, so it gets used to the idea.

HEALTH AND SAFETY

Pet dogs should be vaccinated, neutered and microchipped. A microchip identifies the dog's owner so it can be returned if it gets lost.

NEUTERING

Puppies are usually neutered when they're about six months old and neutered dogs usually make better pets. Neutering prevents certain diseases and stops pets wandering too far from home. Unneutered male dogs are more likely to fight and scent-mark their territories.

Microchips are inserted under the skin between a dog's shoulder blades.

PET CHECK ✓

Has your dog been:

- vaccinated?
- neutered?
- microchipped?

THE GREAT OUTDOORS

Puppies shouldn't go outdoors for walks until two weeks after their final vaccinations, but they still need to learn about the outside world. Try taking your puppy out in a dog carrier, or on a car journey, so it can get used to outdoor sounds and smells.

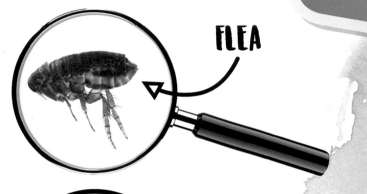

FLEA

TICK

UNWANTED GUESTS

Keep an eye out for fleas and ticks when you groom your dog. They make life miserable for your pet and can cause diseases. There are injections and treatments to get rid of them, so take advice from your vet.

WEIGHT CHECK

Being overweight is one of the biggest risks to a dog's health. Overweight animals often die earlier as it affects their breathing, heart and joints. Here's how to make sure your pet is a healthy weight:

- You should be able to feel your dog's bones beneath a thin layer of fat.

- Your dog should have a narrower waist behind the ribs.

DOG BEHAVIOUR

In the wild, dogs live in packs led by the top dog and every member knows its place. At home, a dog's owner should be 'top dog' and the family is its pack.

YOU ARE THE BOSS

Dog pack leaders control where other dogs sleep, when they eat and when they leave the pack. It's a big responsibility and most dogs don't want the job. Without a strong leader, your dog will feel it has to take control and it will get very cross with members of the family that do as they please and don't stick to its rules.

BETTER AT THE BOTTOM

In your family pack, your dog should be at the bottom. This might sound mean, but if you're a dog, being at the bottom of the pack, cared for and protected by the other members, is a very comfortable place.

HOUSE MANNERS

Top dogs get the best sleeping spot, so if you allow your pet to sit on your sofa or sleep on your bed, it could get the message that it is in charge. If your family doesn't mind sharing the furniture with your dog, make sure it's strictly by invitation only.

SEEING THROUGH THE NOSE

Dogs 'see' the world through their noses. Their sense of smell is so good they can build up a picture with a quick sniff. They will know where you have been, what you have touched, who you met and what you had for lunch.

UNDERSTAND YOUR PET

If you let me know how you want me to behave, I'll do my best to please you.

COMMUNICATION

Dogs often behave as if they understand when we talk to them, but it's more likely that they're reading our body language because that's the main way that dogs communicate.

TAIL TALK

Dogs wag their tail when they're happy, but a wagging tail can have other meanings too:

- A tail that wags so hard it makes the dog's bottom wiggle means the dog is feeling friendly and ready to play.

- A wagging tail accompanied by barking and hard, staring eyes means the dog is frustrated, so move away.

- If a dog yawns or licks its lips when it's not tired or hungry, it's feeling anxious, even though it may be wagging its tail.

- A tail held high and wagging slowly means the dog is assessing a situation.

- If your dog is holding its tail low or between its legs, it's feeling nervous.

BE WARNED

An angry dog will have a stiff, upright body and its hair may stand on end to make it look bigger. Its ears will be back, it will bare its teeth and it may give a threatening growl. This is your warning that it's time to leave quietly and give the dog a chance to calm down, otherwise you may get bitten.

PLEASED TO MEET YOU

When humans meet, they walk straight up to one another and look each other in the eye. Dogs would think this is very rude. They approach side to side and sniff each other's bottoms, which tells them all they need to know about the other dog. Imagine if humans behaved like that!

UNDERSTAND YOUR PET

If I crouch down with my bottom in the air, I'm ready to play.

TRAINING

Start training your puppy as soon as possible. Training should be fun, so don't let your dog get bored. Short training sessions of less than 10 minutes are best. Never punish your dog – it will be frightened of you and less likely to do what you ask.

GOOD DOG!

Dogs want to please, so they should be given lots of praise for doing the right thing. Small tasty treats are a good reward when you first start training, but once your dog has learned what to do, your praise should be enough.

SIT!

ROLL OVER!

TEACHING COMMANDS

Start by teaching your dog to sit. This is a good way to keep your dog safe and stop it running away or jumping up at people.

- Make sure that your dog is concentrating on you.
- Show that you have a treat in your hand.
- Slowly move the treat over your pet's head and say, 'Sit!'
- Your dog should move into the 'sit' position as it tries to reach the treat.
- Hand over the treat and give your dog plenty of praise.
- Repeat this, saying, 'Sit!' each time.
- Hand signals help your dog to understand.

Once your dog has mastered this, you can teach other commands, such as 'Stay!', 'Come!', 'Down!' and 'Roll over!' Always use the same word and tone of voice.

TOILET TRAINING TIPS

- Take your puppy outside first thing in the morning, then every hour.
- Give a treat and lots of praise when your dog goes to the toilet outside, and always pick up any mess.
- Never punish a dog for having an accident indoors.

UNDERSTAND YOUR PET

Only teach me one command at a time and give me a toy to play with when training has finished.

FUN AND GAMES

Dogs like different sorts of games depending on their breed and personality. Here are some games that you and your dog can both enjoy – see which your pet likes best.

TUG OF WAR

Most dogs love to play tug of war with their owners, but only do this with a dog that isn't stronger than you. There are lots of toys designed for this sort of game.

HIDE AND SEEK

You can combine a hide-and-seek game with training your dog to stay and come. Try hiding in another room and calling your dog.

POUNCING GAMES

This sort of game is popular with small dogs that have been bred to hunt prey. Tie a toy, or an old stuffed sock, to a piece of string and pull it along the floor.

MAKE YOUR OWN TOYS

- Put a treat inside a plastic bottle without a lid, or inside a cereal box, and let your dog get it out.

- Plait old T-shirts together to make a tug-of-war toy.

- Tie a tennis ball inside an old T-shirt to make a tossing toy.

CHASE AND RETRIEVE

Some breeds love to chase and retrieve balls, and a ball launcher will help you to throw the ball even farther. You can play this game with a frisbee and other toys, too.

RULES OF PLAY

- Don't play wrestling games with your dog – you might get hurt.

- Rotate toys and games so your dog doesn't get bored.

- Tidy toys away after playing.

- Play in short bursts and stop while your dog is still having fun.

DOG QUIZ

1 How does a dog tell you it wants to play?

a. It rolls over
b. It crouches with its bottom in the air
c. It puts its ears back

2 Why were Dachshunds bred with short legs?

a. So they couldn't run away
b. To stop them climbing on the furniture
c. To hunt badgers

3 Which of these dog breeds is famous for its sense of smell?

a. Yorkshire terrier
b. Greyhound
c. Bloodhound

4 Which breed of dog has webbed feet?

a. Newfoundland
b. Dalmatian
c. Labrador

5 How many meals should an adult dog have each day?

a. 2
b. 3
c. 4

6 Which animals did dogs evolve from?

a. Foxes
b. Wolves
c. Hyenas

10 How is a dog feeling if it is yawning when it's not tired?

a. Happy
b. Relaxed
c. Anxious

7 Why do dogs pant?

a. Because they're hungry
b. To cool down
c. As a warning that they may bite

8 How often should your dog's nails be trimmed?

a. Every day
b. Every week
c. Every month

9 Which of these foods is harmful to dogs?

a. Grapes
b. Carrot
c. Coconut

QUIZ ANSWERS

1 How does a dog tell you it wants to play?

    b. It crouches with its bottom in the air

2 Why were Dachshunds bred with short legs?

    c. To hunt badgers

3 Which of these dog breeds is famous for its sense of smell?

    c. Bloodhound

4 Which breed of dog has webbed feet?

    a. Newfoundland

5 How many meals should an adult dog have each day?

    a. 2

6 Which animals did dogs evolve from?

    b. Wolves

7 Why do dogs pant?

    b. To cool down

8 How often should your dog's nails be trimmed?

    c. Every month

9 Which of these foods is harmful to dogs?

    a. Grapes

10 How is a dog feeling if it is yawning when it's not tired?

    c. Anxious

GLOSSARY

body language – The way humans and animals communicate how they are feeling, or what they are thinking, through their facial expressions, movements and body position.

breed – Named dog breeds have special features, such as a particular body shape or type of fur, and all members of a breed will look more or less the same.

crate – A wire cage with a door. It's a place where a dog can feel safe, and it can be used when travelling by car.

evolve – To slowly develop or change over generations.

flea – A blood-sucking insect that causes itching and may carry diseases.

frustrated – Feeling disappointed or angry about being unable to do something.

gland – Organs that make fluids and chemicals, such as saliva, sweat, scent and tears.

ID tag – A metal badge that is attached to a dog's collar and shows its owner's name, address and telephone number.

Jacobson's organs – Two tube-like organs in the roof of the mouth that recognise chemicals in smells such as urine, as well as chemical signals given by other animals.

microchip – A microchip is a tiny electronic device, the size of a grain of rice. It has a number that is stored on a computer with a record of the owner's name and address. A scanner will show the number so a lost cat's owner can be found.

mixed-breed – A dog that has parents from several different breeds. It is sometimes called a mongrel.

neutering – An operation that stops dogs having puppies. Neutered dogs make better, healthier pets, so it is recommended for males and females.

pack – A group of animals that live and hunt together in the wild.

pedigree dog – A dog that has two pure-bred parents of the same breed.

pet barrier – A gate or pen that keeps a dog separate from other animals or young children.

prey – An animal that is hunted and killed by others.

pure-breed – A dog that has two parents of the same breed.

scavenger – A creature that eats carrion (the flesh of animals that have died). In the wild, dogs are both hunters and scavengers.

scent-marking – Dogs scent-mark their territories with urine to send a message to other dogs. Neutering your puppy will reduce this behaviour.

scent receptors – Cells inside the nose that absorb smells and send information to the brain. Humans have six million scent receptors, but a bloodhound has 300 million.

tick – A tiny creature that is related to a spider. Ticks suck blood and look like warts or blood blisters when they are feeding. They should be removed using a special tool.

vaccination – An injection that protects dogs from serious diseases, such as parvovirus and distemper.

INDEX